YOUTH WITH GENDER ISSUES

Seeking an Identity

HELPING YOUTH WITH MENTAL, PHYSICAL, AND SOCIAL CHALLENGES

Title List

YOUTH WITH GENDER ISSUES

Seeking an Identity

by Kenneth McIntosh
and Ida Walker

Mason Crest Publishers
Philadelphia

Mason Crest Publishers Inc.
370 Reed Road
Broomall, Pennsylvania 19008
(866) MCP-BOOK (toll free)
www.masoncrest.com

First printing

1 2 3 4 5 6 7 8 9 10

ISBN 978-1-4222-0133-6 (series)

Library of Congress Cataloging-in-Publication Data

McIntosh, Kenneth, 1959–

Youth with gender issues : seeking an identity / by Kenneth McIntosh and Ida Walker.

p. cm. — (Youth with special needs)

Includes bibliographical references and index.

ISBN 978-1-4222-0145-9 (alk. paper)

1. Transsexual youth. 2. Transsexualism. 3. Gender identity. I. Walker, Ida. II. Title.

HQ77.9.M35 2008

306.76'80835—dc22

2007006742

Interior pages produced by
Harding House Publishing Service, Inc.
www.hardinghousepages.com
Interior design by MK Bassett-Harvey.
Cover design by MK Bassett-Harvey.
Cover Illustration by Keith Rosko.
Printed in the Hashemite Kingdom of Jordan.

The creators of this book have made every effort to provide accurate information, but it should not be used as a substitute for the help and services of trained professionals.

Contents

Introduction

We are all people first, before anything else. Our shared humanity is more important than the impressions we give to each other by how we look, how we learn, or how we act. Each of us is worthy simply because we are all part of the human race. Though we are all different in many ways, we can celebrate our differences as well as our similarities.

In this book series, you will read about many young people with various special needs that impact their lives in different ways. The disabilities are not *who* the people are, but the disabilities are an important characteristic of each person. When we recognize that we all have differing needs, we can grow toward greater awareness and tolerance of each other. Just as important, we can learn to accept our differences.

Not all young people with a disability are the same as the persons in the stories. But you will learn from these stories how a special need impacts a young person, as well as his or her family and friends. The story will help you understand differences better and appreciate how differences make us all stronger and better.

—*Cindy Croft, M.A.Ed.*

Did you know that as many as 8 percent of teens experience anxiety or depression, and as many as 70 to 90 percent will use substances such as alcohol or illicit drugs at some time? Other young people are living with life-threatening diseases including HIV infection and cancer, as well as chronic psychiatric conditions such as bipolar disease and schizophrenia. Still other teens have the challenge of being "different" from peers because they are intellectually gifted, are from another culture, or have trouble controlling their behavior or socializing with others. All youth with challenges experience additional stresses compared to their typical peers. The good news is that there are many resources and supports available to help these young people, as well as their friends and families.

The stories contained in each book of this series also contain factual information that will enhance your own understanding of the particular condition being presented. If you or someone you know is struggling with a similar condition or experience, this series can give you important information about where and how you can get help. After reading these stories, we hope that you will be more open to the differences you encounter in your peers and more willing to get to know others who are "different."

—*Carolyn Bridgemohan, M.D.*

Chapter 1

Starting Over at Shore View

ye, Mom." I give her a peck on the cheek, wave, and try to smile as I step out of the car, shoulder my backpack, and turn to face the entrance of my new school.

Gotta' be brave for Mom, especially after everything she's gone through the past year. Not just my problems, but the burden of dealing with the Jerk, as well. I can't let her know that this, "chance to start over" feels like facing the firing squad.

When I glance over my shoulder, she's still sitting in the car, looking after me. Neither of us really wants to part; but she's got to be at her job and I've gotta' enter this building before the bell rings. So we both force smiles, wave again, and she puts the car into gear and heads out of the parking lot.

I'm alone.

Totally.

Shore View High. The words are carved in huge block letters on sandstone over the lintel of the school entrance. A portal—the entrance to my new life.

Portals in stories bring transformation. They can send Alice into her fantasy world, Elizabeth Bennet into a ballroom full of exciting new people in a Jane Austen novel, and in mythology, they can lead to heaven or hell. Which will this be? I dream of a place where the other students are sweet and gentle so they won't harass me. Or will it be hell, like my old school?

First stop is the office. I go up to the counter, hand the secretary my ID. She doesn't even look at me, just takes the documents, sits at her computer, and types. Then she tells me to stand on the line and smile toward the digital camera for my school ID picture.

I wish I had on make-up, wish my hair was better arranged. I'm going to look awful plain for this plastic image, but I know that's better. Plain won't attract attention.

Then I sit and wait. Lots of hustle and bustle around me in the office, but I'm in the corner, looking at the floor. I tug at my long sleeves, make sure they cover all the way to my wrists. Keep those arms covered at all times. Students and teachers saunter around the room, but no one sees me. I'm like the fake plant sitting next to me, just a fixture in this environment. Good.

The secretary calls me, hands me my new school ID, locker number and combo, and class schedule. Would I like a map of the school? Sure.

I look down at my new school identification card, encased in shiny clear plastic. That's not really me. I'm glad though; at this new school I prefer to be incognito. Much safer.

I head out the door, into the stream of students rushing hither and yon, greeting one another and preparing for the day. For an instant, I feel dizzy.

Room tilts.

Vertigo.

I see all these people, and I feel like there's a big target on my back.

Just shoot me.

Gotta' breathe. Breathe. Deep breaths.

Tell myself, *You can do this.*

On with the show. I glance at my locker number and the little map; my locker is in a dead-end corner at the end of the hall on the second floor. That's good, actually: away from the main drag. Maybe I'll be alone.

Okay, this is my locker. And no one's here. Today might turn out all right, after all. I look at the combo and start spinning the dials. Nope; won't open. Gotta start over.

"Hello-o-o. Haven't seen you before. Are you new to the school?"

I look up from the spinning dial on my locker, into the most exquisite face imaginable.

Immediately, I'm green with envy.

The girl next to me is Asian, shorter than me by a few inches. She has enormous, dark eyes, perfectly manicured eyebrows, and lips outlined in bright red lipstick. Why can't I be so pretty? She's petite but curvaceous; oh, I wish I had a figure like that. And she's wearing a tight little baby-blue dress over white stockings and shiny blue knee-length boots. You need to have the looks to pull off that kind of wardrobe. This girl has them—I don't.

She smiles, showing me a glittering expanse of white teeth. "I'm Vanna. What's your name?"

I introduce myself quickly, half hoping she won't remember me. Then she wants to know where I'm from, and I tell her, "A little town up the coast."

"What was it like there?"

"All right." Not true, but this isn't time for confessions.

I notice her purse: Betty Boop outlined with sequins. Very nice. I almost comment on it, but then I think better.

Then I hear footsteps behind us, more voices. Vanna is immediately surrounded by a small group of her friends. I'd hoped to have a quiet, out-of-the-way locker, but I am in the wrong spot. Now I hope Vanna will forget me, but again, no such luck. Her lips are moving and she's pointing back and forth between me and her friends. I'm being introduced.

Wish I was in a *Harry Potter* novel, with an invisibility cloak I could wrap around me and vanish into thin-air. It would be so much simpler to live in a fantasy.

". . . this is Tanya," Vanna is saying, gesturing toward a dark-skinned student with short hair, jeans, and T-shirt. She's wearing a silver bracelet with several large chunks of green turquoise. I'm guessing she's Native American. Tanya nods her head and flashes a shy smile at me. She looks harmless; she might even be a possible friend. I make a mental note of her name.

Vanna goes on around the circle. "And this is Josh; we call him 'Boy Wonder.'" They all giggle, and a tall, muscle-bound boy with blue eyes shakes my hand. He practically crushes my palm and fingers; it feels like getting my digits stuck in a tightening vice-grip.

I'm always intimidated by boys, especially apes like this one.

"Pleased to meet ya."

"My pleasure."

Not.

This guy's an Alpha male. I can smell them a mile away. He's probably all macho and full of himself. And he's wearing a big wooden cross around his neck, which means he's one of those fundamentalist types. I'm still sorting out my religious beliefs; from what I can understand, Jesus was pretty cool when it came to not judging people. But I'm leery of anyone who wears his faith around his neck.

Josh gestures toward a slight girl standing close beside him, arm around his waist. "Hello, I'm Ashley," the girl says with a genuine-looking smile. Ashley is a bit less than my height: thin, dressed in faded blouse, jeans, and sneakers. I like her immediately, but I wish she weren't clinging to the big gorilla. Is she not so sweet as she seems, or have I misjudged the guy? Time will tell.

"What's your first class?" Vanna asks.

I glance at my list.

"Mr. Vallencio, Earth Science."

"Oh, you'll like him. He's one of my favorite teachers," Josh says.

"Lots of great discussions—that's mostly all we do in his class," Vanna chimes in.

Discussion classes are the worst. I much prefer lectures and writing assignments. My first day at Shore View isn't turning out so well, and I haven't even started the school day.

"I'm in Earth Science first period. I'll walk you there if you like," Ashley offers.

I'd rather be alone, but I don't want to be rude. I'll need to get acquainted with other students eventually, may as well start now.

I suppose.

Maybe.

I give a noncommittal nod and pick up my backpack. I still haven't gotten the locker open, but I'll figure that out later when I don't have a whole crowd of nosey people surrounding me.

The warning bell rings. Vanna, Josh, and Tanya head separate directions; Ashley and I start walking down the hall.

"Where are you from?" she asks, and I tell her.

"That's on the coast, right?"

"Uh-huh," I reply.

"You surf?"

"Yes, I like being out in the ocean." I want to tell her about my pretty Roxy board, but I bite my lip. Not good to reveal too much too soon.

A stream of students is heading into the door of what is apparently Mr. Vallencio's room. I slip into the flow and choose a vacant seat next to Ashley.

The bell rings again, and the students quiet down.

Mr. Vallencio is a short man with glasses, dark beard and mustache. He announces, "Good morning, class. I have a note from the office, let me see, where is that? Oh yes, here it is. It says we have a new student. Everyone say hello to . . . Kevin Campbell."

I force a smile and wave at my new classmates.

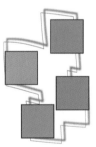

The Difference Between Sex and Gender

First, gender and sex are *not* different words for the same thing, even though the words both deal with male and female. Before the mid-1950s, the word "gender" was used primarily when discussing male and female as they pertained to grammar; in many foreign languages, adjectives and nouns change depending on the gender of what's being discussed (and even inanimate objects possess gender in languages like French and Spanish).

In late 1955, the controversial psychologist John Money coined the phrase "gender role" in an article discussing **hermaphroditism**. In the mid-1960s, a group at the University of California defined "gender

Sex and gender are two different concepts; both are more complex than you might think.

identity." Those were the first instances of the use of the word gender in a non-grammatical context.

An individual's sex is generally known from birth, based on the sexual organs of the newborn. A male baby will have a penis; a female baby will not, instead possessing a uterus, vagina, vulva, and labia. Of course, many parents-to-be can now find out the sex of their child before birth, thanks to **sonograms**. In short, sex is anatomical.

So, What Is Gender?

According to *Merriam-Webster's Collegiate Dictionary* (eleventh edition), gender consists of the behavioral, cultural, or psychological traits typically associated with one sex. This means, of course, that gender is divided into male and female. But wait! What about those individuals who do not consider themselves to be either sex or, in rare cases, to be members of both sexes? Does society just not count them? No, gender is not that simple.

A more accurate representation of gender would be to divide the concept into gender identity and gender role, as it evolved in scientific literature. Briefly put, gender identity is how *we* see ourselves, and gender role is how *others* perceive us.

Gender Identity

According to many experts, gender identity exists in the mind of the individual; it is a psychological concept not necessarily based on biological fact. If someone *believes* he is male, then his gender identity would be male. In most cases, one's gender identity matches his or her biological sex organs—but not always. Some evidence indicates that gender identity may have a

In the United States, most restrooms are labeled for males or
for females, making gender identification a part of a basic bodily
function. In many other countries, including some provinces in
Canada, however, this most basic of sorting systems—whether
one uses the men's room or the ladies'—is not perceived to be
needed, and public bathrooms are usually unisex.

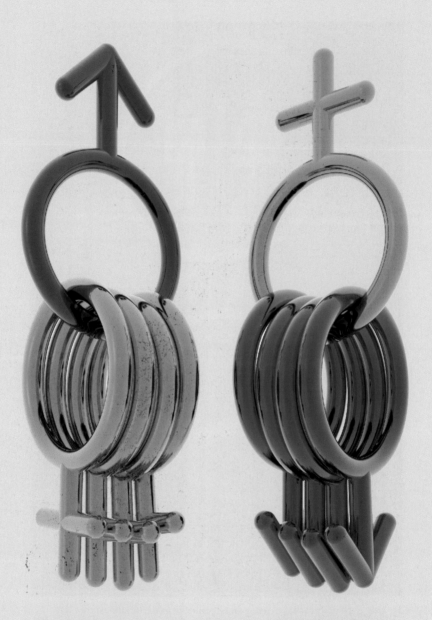

All males have some feminine characteristics and all females have masculine characteristics. In most cases, however, these do not interfere with whether one perceives oneself as primarily male or female.

biological component; organic differences have been found in brain anatomy in those with gender identity disorder.

Gender Role

It's a lesson learned early in life: how we see ourselves is not necessarily the same as how others see us. Someone may consider herself to be female (her gender identity), but others won't confirm that perception until they see her behaving and dressing as they believe a female should.

Behaviors and dress are not the same all over the world. What is behavior or dress characteristic of a male in one part of the world might be characteristic of a female in another. One must take care not to jump to conclusions without knowing all of the facts.

How we see ourselves doesn't always match up with what others perceive from the outside.

Chapter 2
Under the Microscope

evin, welcome to Shore View. We have great teachers, great weather"— the class chuckles—"and, especially, great students"—scattered applause from the class. "I'm sure you'll fit right in here."

Wow, Mr. Vallencio can sure pour on the syrup. Little does he know.

"Alright, class," the teacher continues. "Yesterday we started to discuss the diversity of marine biospheres. Now, if you'll turn to page 243 of your textbook, and refer to the chart on the top of that page..."

I glance around the room. All eyes and noses are stuck in books. Good. I'm no longer the center of attention.

How is this new school going to work out? Too soon to tell. Students look about the same as my old school. Probably all the same types of people: socialites, party girls, athletes, burn-outs, surfers, and geeks. I look at the faces in the room. Is anyone here a kindred spirit? Could any of these people really understand me? So hard to know. The girl sitting next to me could be my soul-mate—but just as likely, she'll end up my worst, most vicious enemy. Humans don't come with warning labels or product guarantees, so there's no telling what you'll get.

Why does life have to be so complicated?

I drift away mentally from Mr. Vallencio's earth science class, back to my first memories of school. Things were okay for the first couple of years. Little kids aren't as hung-up on boys' and girls' respective roles as they are later on. I played house and kickball at recess time; both activities involved both sexes and I fit in okay.

Going shopping, I would look at girls' clothes and say, "Mommy, Daddy, can I have that?"

Mom would say, "No, Kevin, those are girls' clothes. Things for little boys are in this section, over here."

After my dad died, my older brother, Randall, became my nemesis. He quickly caught on that I was a "sissy," and took advantage of what he perceived to be my weaknesses. "What's wrong with you? You're acting like a girl."

Exactly.

That's the story of my life, in a nutshell.

A boy's body with a girl's mind.

Is my soul like a nut stuck in the wrong shell?

Or is the whole world whacked, refusing to treat people like myself with common sense and dignity?

The sound of books slamming shut brings me back to the present moment. "Alright then," Mr. Vallencio announces. "We're going to apply these concepts to an experiment. At the back of the room are samples of water of varying salinity. Compare the density of microscopic populations on a glass slide, and try to come up with a hypothesis about that for your lab notebooks. We don't have enough microscopes for everyone, so some of you will have to work with partners."

Students head for the back of the room, where the experiment materials are. I rush toward a microscope. If I can lay claim to one of my own, maybe I won't need to partner with anyone. Ashley apparently has a partner already; she's sitting down at a 'scope next to a brown-skinned girl in a cheerleading outfit. I'm alone with my 'scope. Good. Unpleasant situation avoided.

I dip a glass slide into a bottle filled with water, place a smaller square pane over that, and slide it beneath the ocular tube. I squint into the eyepiece and look at the tiny organisms swimming in their infinitesimal world. And I imagine myself on the slide, an innocent little creature in a world of confusing and threatening relationships.

My dad died when I was in fourth grade. I remember the funeral, Mom sniffling and daubing her cheeks, Randall and I standing next to her, not fully comprehending. The coffin lowered into the earth; clods of dirt hit the top of the box with a dull thump that makes me shudder to this day.

After that, Mom had to work more—so I was left alone afternoons, left to my brother's tender mercies. Heaven help me. He'd want to play football; I couldn't throw, catch, or tackle well. Sometimes, I'd go into Mom's room and take her clothes out of the closet, just to feel their silky softness and admire the colors. Randall would call me all kinds of names and laugh at me.

When I could, I'd go next door and play with our neighbor, Samantha. She was my best playmate as a little child, and even when things became awful in junior high, she defended me in the face of our peers. We played Barbie or dress-up, and I was relaxed and happy. But it didn't last.

Samantha's mother apparently had words with my mom, because one evening she sat me down and gave me a long talk about "boy things" as opposed to "girl things." She sounded like I was confused, as if I didn't know the difference. She didn't find my response very reassuring: I told her I knew about boy things and girl things. I was really a girl; I just looked like a boy. I was sure that some day soon my private parts would fall off and my chest would get bigger and everyone else would realize I was a girl, as well. Ah, the innocence of children.

I even knew my "real" name—Kendra. I'm not sure where that came from, but it still makes sense to me. The name on my school identification card, driver's license, and birth certificate—Kevin—is how the world sees me, but inside I'm Kendra.

Mom grew more concerned. She took me to see a doctor. He asked me a slew of questions, furrowed his brow as I answered, and scribbled words on a notepad. Then I was asked to wait outside; I could hear hushed, earnest words exchanged inside the office. "Boy is very confused . . . loss of his father . . . possibly homosexual . . ."

Mom undertook a zealous campaign to "straighten out" my confusion. She took me to a boys' club: it was awful. The other boys scared me, and they sensed my anxiety like a pack of wolves sniffing out a defenseless lamb. My first campout, they tied me to a tree, and I was left alone for more than an hour until the scoutmaster came and found me. I peed myself, alone in the woods, frightened. The other boys smirked and winked, called me names. I came home from the campout traumatized, and Mom didn't make me go to boys' clubs any more after that.

But the "manhood" campaign was just beginning. My brother was enlisted to assist in teaching me masculinity; I was forced to go with him and other slightly older neighborhood boys to their ball games, BB gun fights, and so on. I stunk at all those activities. While Randall was allegedly "helping" me, he would side with the other boys in making fun of me.

Worst, Mom found a new love interest. The Jerk moved in with us. I will never to the end of my days understand what Mom saw in that man; my own memories are of undistilled meanness. I am afraid she thought I needed a father figure, a masculine presence under the roof. If that was her intention, she was tragically mistaken.

For five awful years, I listened to that man yelling—at me, at Mom, at Randall. He floated from job to job, sat around the house and drank, watched games on the television, and turned our orderly apartment into a grungy mess. But maybe that was worth it in Mom's eyes, because he punished every tendency toward "faggy" behavior on my part. Twice, he caught me trying on Mom's clothes, and several times I borrowed Samantha's dolls to play with at my house. When I did those things, he screamed at me so bad I cried. Then he beat me. That was way more than Mom had asked for or wanted—but if she tried to interfere, he'd yell at Mom, acting as if it was all her fault.

By my freshman year in high school, I'd adopted a strange sort of gender neutrality. Mom, the Jerk, and Randall had succeeded in "conditioning" Kendra to behave more like Kevin—or more accurately, some sort of sexless being between the two. I wore my hair long, and draped myself in loose-fitting, style-less threads that could pass for boy's or girl's clothes. I distanced myself from others, refusing to hang around with Randall's crowd any longer. Samantha was my only real friend.

Fortunately, Samantha started hanging out with the surfer crowd, a group that included both sexes. I've always been slight, but I was sturdy enough to master swimming out on a board, diving through swells, and balancing on the curls.

The ocean is like a soothing mother that makes no judgments; she's so huge and yielding that she accepts all her children just as they are. I can be at peace on a glassy day, kneeling on my board and soaking in sunlight, or riding gentle waves, swooshing in toward the shore. Of course, a lot of surfer males are the worst sort of machismo—but I kept to myself, and steered away from conversations that would lead to ribbing.

"Well, Kevin, what sorts of conclusions have you reached?" It's Mr. Vallencio, moving along the rows of students with their experiments, interrupting my memories.

"Uh, there seems to be an inverse ratio between salinity and density of organisms in the water."

The teacher smiles. "Very good, Kevin, I can see you'll do well in this course."

He moves on to the pair of kids next to me. Is the class really this simple? Why are we doing experiments to prove such an obvious point?

As I start to clean up the slides, my mind wanders. . . .

The onset of my life's crisis was Samantha's first date. She was giddy over her new boyfriend, and as I listened to her, I realized that I could not avoid dealing with my gender issues forever. It was the start of junior year, and I was feeling stronger, more rebellious. I could stand up for myself—or so I thought.

Other events propelled this season of change in my life. One was the increase in the tension between Mom and the Jerk. He had always yelled at her—but now she was finding strength within herself to yell back at him. That made things louder, scarier, more unpredictable—but I was proud of Mom for standing up to him. I hoped she might drive him out of the house. Eventually, that happened.

At the same time, I found an unlikely advocate: my brother! Randall started taking classes at UC, including a course titled Sex, Gender and Society. He came home one weekend from school, sat us all down at the dining room table, and announced, "Kevin's all right. It's the world that's screwed up." Then he looked at me and said, "Kevin—or Kendra, if you want me to call you that—I've been treating you like crap. I'm sorry. I just didn't understand." I don't think I've ever felt such love for anyone as I did for my brother that instant.

He then rambled on for the next hour about transgender people, the brain, human psyche, and so on. The Jerk just glared at him, Mom sat wide-eyed, but for me it was validation—the first I'd felt in a long time.

The next few months blur in my memory; as Dickens might say, it was the best and worst of times. Buoyed by the changes in my family, I decided to stand up to the world and declare my real self. I confided to a few friends at school that I was really Kendra, not Kevin—always had been and always will be. I bought new clothes that I really wanted, including some pastels.

The biggest thing was—I bought the surfboard I'd been coveting. Until then, I rode a black thruster that I got at a yard sale, dark, menacing, masculine. But on a glorious sunny day I walked into the Roxy store and came out with seven feet of sparkling new fiberglass, the top artfully covered in a pink hibiscus pattern. I can hardly convey how good it felt to race out into the waves and jump on that board, paddling out to sea on a vessel that proclaimed the real me.

But I was still innocent, as naive as the day years earlier when I'd told Mom I was really a girl, I just looked like a boy, and expected her to understand and accept that.

The proverbial you-know-what hit the fan at my old school.

For the most part, I was ostracized. Treated like I didn't exist. The girls wouldn't have anything to do with me—and neither would the guys. Only Samantha stood up for me. Then one terrible day she gave in as well and joined my tormenters. I was alone. Home was no refuge, either: the battles between Mom and the Jerk were relentless, sometimes violent.

In the middle of this mayhem and desolation, I became bitter. I needed to lash out; I wanted to return pain for pain. So where did I direct my anger? At my own body. I hate the way it refuses to listen to my mind, growing facial hair that repulses me, staying flat on top where I should have breasts. So I took out my anger with razor blades and paring knives, cutting my arms and legs when no one watched. The cutting gave me an odd feeling of euphoria.

Of course, Mom found out. I was sent to a clinic, where I spent several weeks until I swore up and down not to cut myself again.

When I returned home, the Jerk was gone; Mom had won the war for our household. Then, Mom announced the big move to Huntington Beach. A new job for her, and the "opportunity to start on a new foot" for me.

So here I am, sitting in Mr. Vallencio's Earth Science class at Shore View High.

As confused as ever.

More frightened than before.

For years, I've tried to be Kevin, but I've never been comfortable inside my own skin. At my old school, I tried to come out as Kendra, that didn't work either. So who am I? Where do I fit in? And how can I forge an identity and survive here at this new school?

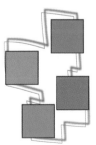

The Physiology of Gender

Although gender and sex are not the same things, one's gender development does begin in the womb with the development of physical characteristics that influence how the child will be treated after birth. After all, in most cases, there is a direct **correlation** between one's gender and one's sex.

All human fetuses begin as female. It is not until the eighth week of pregnancy that male characteristics begin to develop. If the fetus has a Y chromosome and a functional level of testes-determining factor (a gene product), then testes will develop. As **testosterone** levels increase, some of the testosterone will become dihydrotestosterone, a hormone responsible for the development of secondary sex characteristics in males. If for some reason the fetal testes do not produce testosterone, the fetus will continue to develop as a female, even though a Y chromosome is present.

As levels of testosterone and other male hormones increase, the fetus produces other hormones that will stop the development of physical characteristics generally associated with females. Female genitalia will not develop, and the brain's **corpus callosum**,

Fast Fact

X chromosome + X chromosome = female
X chromosome + Y chromosome = male

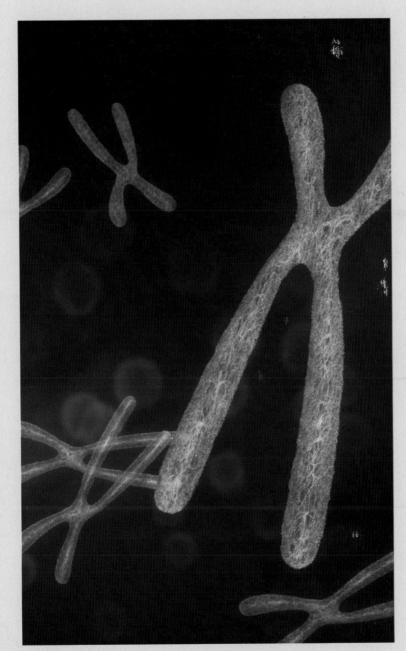

Sex is determined by our chromosomes.

The differences between the sexes have long been viewed as mysterious and powerful forces. Research indicates that in fact women's brains are different from men's.

amygdala, *cerebellum*, and **hypothalamus** will be smaller than those found in males.

Although sex is established before birth, thereby planting the seeds of gender identity, it is not until after birth that one identifies with a specific sex group.

Gender Identity:
The First Steps

For many parents today, the surprise of finding out if their child is male or female comes earlier than birth, due to the increased use of ultrasound machines. Although initially used to detect problems prenatally, the use of this technology is now almost routine. Ultrasound images can still help detect development problems, but they are also used to measure the fetus and let the parents know whether they'll be having a boy or girl. Once parents, friends, and family members know the child's sex, clothing and toys are purchased, many with a specific gender bias. Even the decorating of the nursery and certainly the selection of potential names can be influenced by the newborn's sex. The stage is set for the development of gender identity in the child.

Within each culture, and even each family unit, preconceived ideas exist about what it means to be male or female. As soon as the baby is born, the individuals with whom the child has contact will treat it as they believe a child of that particular sex should be treated. Parents tend to cuddle and hold female children more than males. Assertive play is often encouraged in male children. In most cases, but not all, that treatment will be based on the physical sex of the child.

Growing Up Female?

Dr. John Money was a pioneer in the field of sexual identity and sexual behavior. He studied the subject when there was very little research being conducted on how it developed. Unfortunately, despite the inroads he made into the subject, his name and career will be forever linked with the sad and tragic story of David Reimer.

On August 22, 1965, Janet and Ron Reimer of Winnipeg, Manitoba, Canada, became the parents of healthy, identical twin boys. Bruce and Brian Reimer had no physical problems until the age of eight months, when they were diagnosed with phimosis, an abnormal narrowing of the opening in the foreskin of the penis. To avoid a potential lifetime of infections and irritations, the parents agreed to have both boys **circumcised**. Something went horribly wrong during Bruce's surgery. The surgeon had used a machine that was not approved for such a procedure, and the baby's penis was burned so badly that it couldn't be repaired. (Brian's surgery was immediately canceled.)

Options were limited for the Reimer family in the late 1960s. They visited many doctors, but none could provide them with the hope that their son could live a sexually normal life. Then Dr. John Money entered the picture.

Sitting at home one evening, Janet Reimer saw a television program about the pioneering psychologist. Dr. Money, working at Johns Hopkins University in

Baltimore, Maryland, believed that gender identity could be changed during a child's early life. According to Dr. Money, gender identity was determined by nurture, not nature. The Reimers took their young son to see Dr. Money, and he gave them the hope they had been seeking. At the encouragement of Dr. Money, twenty-one-month-old Bruce had his testicles removed, received hormone treatments, and left the hospital as a girl named Brenda.

Janet did what she could to raise Bruce as Brenda. She dressed him in dresses, styled his hair like that

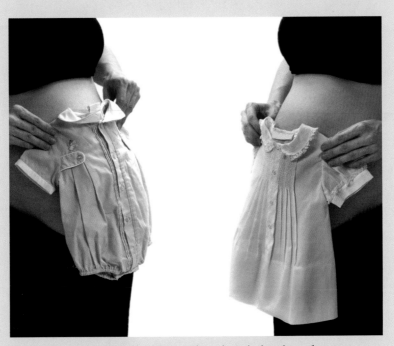

Most pregnant mothers assume that their babies' genders are already determined, even before birth—but that is not always the case.

Male and female roles are some of the most basic divisions found in human society.

of a little girl, and even taught him how to wear makeup. She tried to teach him to act like a "little lady." That wasn't enough though. Brenda didn't like playing with other girls, and she certainly didn't act like one. Instead of behavior that might be expected of a little girl, Brenda got into numerous fights, often caused by the teasing she received for how she walked. Things got so bad that Brenda didn't want to go to school.

By the time Brenda reached age nine, it was obvious that things were not going as Dr. Money had told the Reimer family they would. But if someone read the many articles and books he wrote about Brenda/Bruce (known as the Joan/John case in scientific literature), the opposite would appear to have been the case. The doctor basked in the limelight as he told the story and became a media darling. Dr. Money reported that the transformation had been a success; the one-time male was living a completely adjusted life as a female. Since Brian was still male, the doctor used him as a control, against which he supposedly compared the behavior of Brenda. According to Dr. Money's report, Brenda (Bruce/Joan/John) behaved like a little girl, nothing like how Brian behaved. Family members would dispute the report; during one interview, Brian said that the only difference between he and his twin had been that "he [Bruce] had longer hair."

As the twins hit **puberty**, something was increasingly different about Brenda. Despite developing breasts because of the hormone treatment, she also developed characteristically masculine broad shoulders and muscles on her arms. Problems with school continued, and in an interview with a New York journalist, Janet reported that students wouldn't let Brenda use the male or female restrooms. When the family confronted Dr. Money with their doubts about continuing the charade, he tried to convince them to allow surgeons to operate on Brenda to provide her with a vagina, which hopefully would help her feel more like a female. When approached with the suggestion, thirteen-year-old Bruce had had enough. He threatened to commit suicide if he were made to see Dr. Money. Then, for the first time, his father told Bruce the truth.

Bruce had always known he was different; he just didn't know why. One of his first thoughts was to kill the doctor responsible for performing his circumcision. Instead, he attempted suicide and spent time in a coma. At age fifteen, Brenda was left behind. So was Bruce. In their place was David, dressing and acting like a male. Eventually, mastectomies would remove the breasts, and he would take testosterone injections. **Phalloplasty** would provide him with a functioning penis, but he would not be able to father children. He met a woman, fell in love, and married her, becoming stepfather to her children.

Happy ending? No.

Brian was not immune from the effects of Dr. Money's treatment of his twin. He never really came to terms with what had happened to his family, and he spent much of his life suffering from psychological problems. In 2002, he committed suicide.

As for Bruce/Brenda/David, the happiness he found as a male didn't last. He lost his job, he saw problems between his parents, and he separated from his wife. Then there was his brother's suicide. According to his mother, he never truly recovered from his brother's death, and on May 5, 2004, David also committed suicide.

And what happened to Dr. Money? Once the truth came out about the abysmal failure of the Joan/John experiment, he lost much of the credibility he had gained. According to some who knew him, during his later years, the doctor regretted what he had done, as well as its aftermath. Dr. Money died in July 2006, one day short of his eighty-fifth birthday.

Chapter 3
So Not Paradise

o far, so good. I've made it through my first hour at Shore View without any hassles. Earth science is dismissed and I'm back in the hallway navigating to my next class. This one is called History of Film, and I'm hoping there will be students with intelligent, liberal views. One can always dream.

Entering the room, I see Tanya, the girl Vanna introduced before school. She looks pretty safe, so I sit in the chair next to her. The dark-skinned cheerleader with curly hair comes in, and I notice she has greenish eyes. She's escorted by a wiry fellow with muscular physique and an ominous, beady-eyed look. They sit a few rows in front of me.

Our teacher is Mrs. Kwan, a young woman who looks to be just out of college—not much older than the rest of us. For the first thirty minutes, we watch the finale of John Ford's old black-and-white Western, *Stagecoach*. When the projection ends, Mrs. Kwan rolls up the screen and we talk about the film.

The cheerleader, whom the teacher calls Jada, begins discussion. "I thought it was a great film about breaking down stereotypes. The society woman, the prostitute, the bootlegger, and the gentleman—they discover they're really all the same inside."

"What? Are you kidding?" Tanya interjects. She doesn't even raise her hand, she's so eager to have her say. This girl has more chutzpah than I assumed she would. "My Great-grandpa Peshlaki was one of those whooping Indians in the last scene," she continues. "All you see is mindless, warlike savages. There's nothing about our beautiful Diné culture, no explanation of why those people defended their land against exploitation."

The ominous-looking fellow in front of me has his hand up. Mrs. Kwan calls on him with apparent reluctance. "You have something to say, Cain?"

He turns around to face Tanya. "I'm sick of all the politically correct talk. If your ancestors weren't such wusses, they'd still own this land. It's like in sports—those that can't win, whine."

The Native girl is practically jumping out of her seat, coming back at him with a no-holds-barred retort. This class is proving to be more interesting than I thought it would be.

I admire Tanya—and I'm a little jealous. She isn't afraid to identify herself as a member of a minority, and she's eloquent in the defense of her heritage. I wonder: will there come a day when transgender teens have the same confidence to speak for ourselves? Or are we just too tiny a minority to gain acceptance? Or is it just me—am I too timid to speak up for myself, so I make excuses by blaming the whole of society?

Mrs. Kwan focuses her gaze on me. "What about our new student? Kevin, would you like to add anything to the discussion?"

I'm still thinking about gender issues and minority rights and why we're afraid to speak up, but I *am* afraid, so I quickly make up an inconsequential topic. "I thought it was interesting how the landscape itself plays a role in the movie."

Mrs. Kwan seems pleased with that, "Ah yes. There's a vital role the background adds to the drama of Ford's films."

Then Tanya jumps into the discussion again. Apparently, she has a whole clan of relatives living near Monument Valley where the film was made, and I sit back to listen and relax again.

I'm so good at diverting attention, I amaze myself. I should write a book, *One Hundred Ways to Talk Your Way Out of Any Situation*. The subtitle will be, *My Life as a Teenage Chameleon*.

The bell rings, and I glance again at my schedule of classes.

Uh, oh.

P.E.

Since junior high, I have hated physical education. It's not that I'm so bad at athletics. No, the worst part is the locker room. The boys have an easy-going way of dressing and undressing; they joke and share a camaraderie that feels completely alien to me. I try to hide in the corner, make myself tiny, invisible.

It just feels terribly *wrong* to be with a bunch of naked people of the opposite sex. They may not see it that way— of course, on the outside, I look like any other boy—but I know who I am on the inside, and that makes all the difference.

I walk slow as I can, but in the end, I have to push open the gymnasium doors and report to the locker room. Cain, the ominous one from film class, is in the center of the room, half-naked, snapping towels with the other boys and whooping it up.

I sneak around them toward the stalls.

I'm mindful of another thing—my scars. They're up and down my arms and legs. I don't want to have to explain to a whole room full of merciless males why I've got horizontal markings like a set of railroad tracks covering my limbs. So I slip into a stall and open my backpack, taking out a pair of long-legged sweat pants and a long-sleeved T-shirt.

I've just pulled them on when the door swings violently open. Shoot, I forgot to bolt it shut. There stands Cain. "Hey, guys, look at this," he bellows.

Two of his companions jump to his side. They have me trapped.

"Get a load of that outfit. It's a freak show," Cain exclaims.

I'm shaking; I know I must be turning red. The room starts to spin and I grab the side of the stall. "Please, leave me alone, I'm not bothering you."

He guffaws. "You must be a frickin' queer," he proclaims. "I hate queers."

"Leave me alone." I'm frightened and that makes my voice go even higher than normal. The three boys laugh, and Cain mimics my plea. " 'Leave me alone'—you heard the faggot."

My legs collapse underneath me, and I sit down abruptly on the toilet seat. The three leer at me. What happens now?

I once made the mistake of watching *Boys Don't Cry.* Is this scene going to go down like that? I also read transgender Internet sites and every week there are horrific articles: "Transgender Teen Found Dead in Car" or "Mississippi Killing May Be Gender-Related Hate Crime." So I have nightmares about moments like this. It's like I'm a Jew in Germany, and these guys are the Gestapo. I don't expect much more mercy than that.

"Hey, what are you boys doing there? It's time to get out on the floor." It's the teacher, Coach Steele.

The three amble off, shooting wicked glances at me over their shoulders. I sit back and breathe slowly, regaining composure, taking back control of my limbs.

The locker room is silent now.

I head for the field, where the rest of the class is doing jumping jacks.

"Football today," Coach Steele announces.

Great.

There must be a dark cloud over my head this morning.

They choose up teams. Surprisingly, I'm not last. Some kid even skinnier than me, Jason is his name, he gets that honor.

My team goes off to huddle. Cain looks at me with a predatory grin and says, "I think we should let the new kid be quarterback."

I try to protest, but I know it's a lost cause. This is a set-up. I'm the only kid on this field looking all dorky in long sweats. I stick out like a sore thumb, a sore thumb that's about to get hammered.

The teams line up; the ball comes to me. I toss it away as fast as I can, not even looking where I throw, just so I won't get tackled. But then a half-dozen big guys pummel into me, even *after* the ball's away from my hand and in the air. It's not a football game; it's beat-up-the-weird-kid day.

It happens again.

And again.

All my joints ache, I'm getting hit so hard.

I cast a pleading look at Coach Steele. "What's wrong with you, Campbell?" he shouts. "Goodness sake, boy, take it like a man." I can't believe it. He's in on this scheme. This teacher is just as much a bully as the boys in his class.

Shore View is hell.

Black and blue all over, I've somehow survived PE. Now I'm in the cafeteria, alone in a corner, praying that Cain and his pack of thugs don't eat lunch the same time I do.

Then I see her.

Headed straight toward me.

Green eyes, dark skin, cheerleader's mini-skirt.

It's Cain's girlfriend.

What's her name?

"Hi, I'm Jada." She slips into the bench next to me. I instinctively scoot away.

"You're Cain's girl." I say it as an accusation.

She nods, swivels her head around furtively. Is she looking for her boyfriend? Is she afraid to see him for some reason?

She leans in toward me, and I catch a whiff of her perfume. Lotus Essence, I recognize—very nice taste.

"I'm sorry," she says.

"Huh?"

"What the boys did in PE. I heard Cain talking. You don't deserve that."

"But you're his. . ."

"S-s-h-h." She puts her finger to her lips, leans close to my ear. "I'm sorry. I know he can be a bully. I'm afraid of him, too."

I look in her eyes. Is this a trick? I'd like to trust this girl; goodness knows I can use an ally at this school. But she's a cheerleader—and they're the worst. There wasn't a kind soul in the squad at my old school. If she knew who I am. . . well, their kind are the meanest toward people like me.

She goes on, whispering in my ear. "If things get bad here, I want you to know there's an adult you can talk to— Ms. Torres, the counselor. She can keep secrets. She cares. You can trust her."

Suddenly the cheerleader leaps away from me, as if she has just touched an electric fence. She sees a pair of cheerleaders walking into the cafeteria in their outfits. She puts on a ditzy, cheerful voice—"Hello girls"—and glides away in their direction.

So this is my one friend at this school.

Lucky me.

I'm halfway through day one, and I can already see what lies ahead in this awful place. Kevin is going to be the school laughingstock and punching bag. Can you imagine what they would do if they knew Kevin is really Kendra?

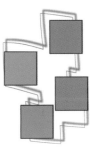

Dolls are often the foundation of gender identity for little girls, who are encouraged to play with them—while little boys are often given trucks and cars to play with instead of dolls.

Gender Role and Gender Identity

How a child is treated by others greatly influences all facets of the child's self-image. Generally, the gender with which the child identifies matches the one indicated by how others treat him based on their perception of his sexual identity. By the age of two or three, most children have accepted their gender identity. For most children, however, it is not until the age of five that they have accepted their gender roles.

Peer groups and family members reinforce gender roles, and this is especially true during the individual's early development. As children mature into adolescents, their world expands as they are exposed to new things, including different cultures. Their sense of what are "gender-appropriate" behaviors and dress may change. This does not mean a change in their gender identity. It is simply a broadening of their ideas of what is acceptable and comfortable.

Chromosomes and Gender

As mentioned previously, females contain XX chromosomes and males XY chromosomes. Cells in most individuals contain forty-six matched pairs of chromosomes. Sometimes this genetic recipe lacks an ingredient or two, or perhaps has too many of one. In those cases, gender identity is not always so clear-cut. Two of the more common conditions are Turner syndrome and Klinefelter syndrome.

Turner Syndrome

When an X chromosome is missing, leaving only another X chromosome, the child is born with an XO chromosomal identity, called Turner syndrome (TS). (Life is not possible with only a Y chromosome.) According to the Turner Syndrome Society (www.turnersyndrome.org), TS occurs in 1 in 2,000 live births and in as many as 10 percent of miscarriages.

Although the baby's external genitalia are female, the ovaries will not develop normally; secondary sex characteristics may not develop and the individual will be infertile. Individuals with Turner syndrome are generally shorter than what is considered normal for women and have webbed necks and broad chests. Most experience physical problems such as heart defects, **hypothyroidism**, and kidney problems. While overall intelligence levels fall within the scientifically defined normal levels, individuals with TS often have difficulty with spatial relationships, nonverbal memory, and attention.

There are some medical treatments that can be helpful for those with TS. Growth hormone therapy can help individuals with TS achieve near-normal height. Estrogen therapy can stimulate the development of secondary sex characteristics. Psychotherapy and participation in support groups can help individuals deal with the physical and emotional aspects of living with TS.

Klinefelter Syndrome

Individuals born with Klinefelter syndrome, also called 47XXY, have at least two X chromosomes and

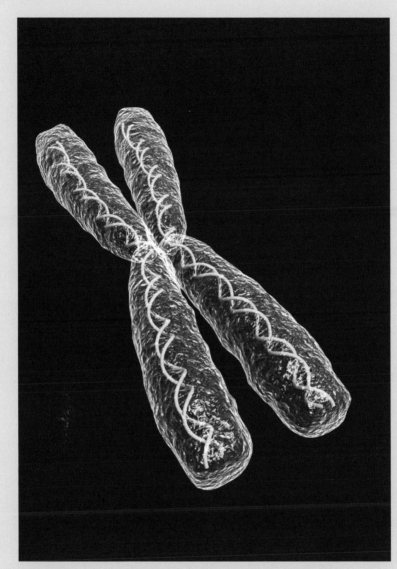

The genetic material contained within an X chromosome is essential to life. When a baby is born with two X chromosomes, she is a girl; when a baby has an X and a Y, he is a boy; and when one chromosome is missing or if there is more than one X chromosome, genetic anomalies will occur, such as Turner and Klinefelter syndromes.

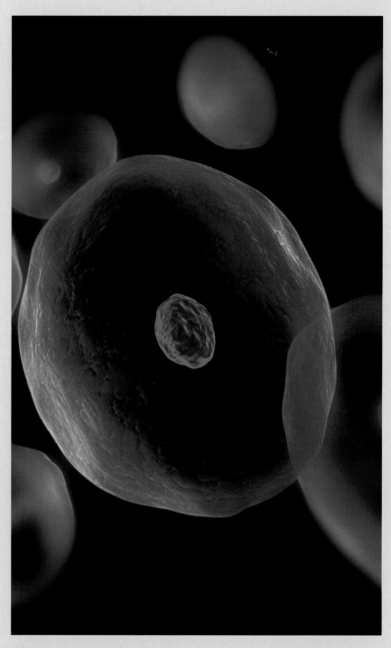

Chromosomes are found within the nucleus of our cells.

one Y chromosome. Klinefelter syndrome occurs in approximately 1 in 500 live male births.

Despite the fact that there are more X chromosomes in the cell nucleus, the Y chromosome means that male sexual organs will be present. Klinefelter syndrome causes underdeveloped testes, and this means that most individuals with this condition will be infertile. While males with Klinefelter syndrome will most likely be taller than the average male, their bodies will take on a feminine appearance. As the child enters puberty, he will often develop enlarged breasts and have low testosterone levels.

Intelligence levels of males with Klinefelter syndrome are sometimes slightly lower than those of non-affected siblings. They may also exhibit problems in speech and hearing. Although individuals with Klinefelter syndrome are male, and assume male gender roles, physical appearance can lead some with the disorder to question their gender identity. Psychotherapy can be helpful for those with this condition.

Chapter 4

Kendra Campbell's Attempted Day Off

ye, Mom."

"Good-bye, Kevin. Have a good day, honey."

I try to smile as I exit the car; it's much harder today than yesterday. Then I feared what might await me; today I know—and I'm terrified.

I stand in the roadside, wave at her until she's out of sight.

I turn toward the school.

Shore View High. The words are still there carved in huge block letters on sandstone over the lintel of the school entrance. Now, I know what this portal is—the gaping maw of hell itself, like something from Dante's *Inferno*, a devouring trap, waiting to chew up and spit out any teen-ager unlucky enough to be uncertain about her identity.

I try to step toward that entrance, but my legs won't obey. There's something wired inside of me, an instinct for self-preservation that won't allow me to walk toward certain sacrifice.

I have never ditched school.

Until today.

I turn and start the long walk toward home.

Half an hour later, I'm there. I collapse onto the sofa, stare at all the junk still unpacked in the house. Standing against a box in the middle of the room is my old black thruster, fins and leash all attached, ready for the ocean. Next to it is my cherished Roxy board, sunlight bouncing off the pink hibiscus pattern on top. It's a nice day out there; maybe I'll feel better if I get some exercise.

I reach for the Roxy board, think better. I'm probably not the only kid skipping school today, no point making things worse. Kevin is having a hard enough time, without being seen on Kendra's surf board.

I slip on a three-quarter wet-suit and pull my beach cruiser bicycle out of the garage. It has a board-holder welded onto the back, and I slip the black board into it. Then I pedal down to the beach, chain the bike to a rack near the pier, and head for the water.

The waves are coming in evenly timed swells, sets of three or four, about waist high. Very nice. I paddle out, duck-dive under the first wave of a set, and catch the next one in. There's plenty of room in the waves today; just me and one other surfer out here, a red-headed boy about my age.

I scoot my board into the crest of the wave, pop up and feel that good surge as I quickly correct, balance, and shoot along the curl.

Sweet.

Life in Huntington Beach might not be so bad after all.

"You're goin' too slow—move it!"

An elbow smashes into my rib.

Pain. Double-over pain.

Wipe out.

I'm flying in the air, leash catches the board, then I'm headfirst into the briny drink and I choke on the water and come up for air.

Wham.

Two of the three fins catch me in the forehead.

And my side's killing me.

My board comes scooting back. I drag my hurting body onto it and drift into shore.

"Locals only. Go back where you came from!" the red-headed boy yells.

What is it? Do I have a tattoo on my back, that only others can see, that says, "Hit me?" How do these creeps always find me? It's like they can smell my vulnerability a mile away.

I stagger out of the water, holding my side with one hand and my board with another. Then I hobble toward my bike and begin the long ride home.

I'm just outside of the Main Street shopping area when a black and white police cruiser pulls up beside me, puts on the siren. The cop motions me to pull over, the car comes to a stop by the curb, and the officer steps out. "You look a little young to be out of school today. Do you have some ID on you?"

I shake my head.

"Truant?"

I'm used to masking my identity, but I'm not-so-good at deceiving authority figures. I decide not to chance it.

"Yes, Officer."

"What's your name?"

"Kevin Campbell."

"School?"

"Shore View."

"Alright then, Kevin. I'm going to phone up your school office and tell them you'll be there in an hour. You bike home, get changed, and go into school where you belong. And don't let me catch you ditching again, alright?"

I nod and do as the officer says.

An hour later, I walk into the school office. The secretary tells me to wait before going to class: Ms. Torres would like to speak with me. I'm escorted into a smaller office beside the main one.

"You can close the door, Kevin," says a neatly dressed Latina as she rises from behind her desk and gestures toward a comfy looking chair.

I sit down as she introduces herself. "I'm Ms. Torres."

I knew that.

"Second day here and ditching already?"

There's no good reply to that one.

"Makes me wonder . . . what happened that was so bad on your first day?"

I focus on the carpeted floor. Her question's taken me by surprise, but I don't feel like talking.

"You came from Pine Cove, up above Frisco, right?"

I wring my hands, noticing how thin and frail my fingers look in the muted light of this tiny room.

"How did you like school there?"

I shrug.

The silence stretched out forever. Finally, I glance up and see her looking in a manila folder; they must have already sent my records from the old school.

"It says here that you had 'serious problems coping with peer relationships' your last semester at Pine Cove High."

I still don't feel like replying.

"And it also says that you asked your friends to call you 'Kendra,' beginning December of last year."

I glance at her sharply. "It says that in my records?"

"Yes." Her voice is gentle. "Would you like me to call you Kevin or Kendra?"

My head is a swirl of emotions. Can I trust this woman? Jada said to, but she's a cheerleader—and her boyfriend is a thug. Ms. Torres seems kind enough; I've learned to scent hypocrisy a ways off, and there's no whiff of that in this office. But then, everything I've done since walking in the door at Shore View seems to bring trouble. So can I believe my inclination to trust this counselor?

I decide to take the defensive approach. "Are you making fun of me?"

I look in her eyes. She looks back, right into my soul. Shakes her head.

I sigh, let all the tension out in a long, exhaled breath, feel my fists unclench and release the flock of butterflies I've been holding in my stomach. "I . . . I'd like you to call me . . . I don't know, Ms. Torres. I'm confused."

I put my eyes in my hands. There's moisture coming out of them onto my palms. "I . . . I'm glad you asked. Really. I'm Kendra—that's the genuine me. But, last time I started telling people that. . ." My throat chokes shut.

Ms. Torres finishes the thought for me, "Last time you tried to assert your female identity, it caused all sorts of problems with your peers."

I nod.

"So you understand yourself as a girl, but the consequences of that are too fearful to make public."

"Yes."

"Well, how about I call you Kendra in this office, but you'll be Kevin outside the door—as long as that's what you want."

I raise my head. "That would be nice. You can do that?"

"Of course."

"Thanks."

"Think nothing of it. Now, I gather you're having problems at this school?"

"My whole life's a problem. It's so confusing. You can't even imagine."

"You're right. I can't know what it feels like living in your skin. But if you tell me, I'll at least have some idea. And I'll listen and try to understand the best I can."

An hour later, I step back outside Ms. Torres' door. I haven't talked to anyone so openly in my whole life, except for Mom and Randall. I have at least one sympathetic ear in this place, so maybe I can survive.

Maybe.

It's not unusual for adolescents to experiment with clothes and hair in extreme ways. Dressing like a Goth girl does not necessarily mean this young man has gender identity disorder; instead, he may merely be expressing his rebellion against mainstream culture or enjoying the shock value of his "look."

When Confusion Exists: Gender Identity Disorder

Sometimes children, and even adolescents, like to dress in the clothing of the opposite sex. No one really knows why this happens. During puberty, a time of major change in an individual's body and life, it is not uncommon for questioning about gender to occur. This is a normal part of exploring identity. In some cases, it goes beyond questioning.

Gender Identity Disorder (GID)

In most cases, when young children dress and behave in ways most would attribute to the other sex, it's

When a young girl dresses like a boy and enjoys "boyish" activities, she is called a tomboy—but a boy who dresses like a girl and likes to play "girly" games is considered a sissy. This disparity reflects the gender bias present in North American society.

A transvestite is someone who dresses in a way appropriate to the opposite sex. This may or may not be because the person has gender identity disorder.

just a passing phase. For some, however, it is a sign that they may have gender identity disorder (GID), a psychological disorder. It is a relatively new diagnostic category that first appeared in the **Diagnostic and Statistical Manual of Mental Disorders**, third edition (DSM-III) in 1980. According to the most recent edition, DSM-IV-TR, specific criteria must be present in the individual before the diagnosis of GID can accurately be made:

A. A strong persistent cross-gender identification (not merely a desire for any perceived cultural advantages of being the other sex). In children, the disturbance is manifested by four (or more) of the following:

- Repeatedly stated desire to be, or insistence that he or she is, the other sex.

- In boys, preference for cross-dressing or simulating female attire; in girls, insistence on wearing only stereotypical masculine clothing.

- Strong and persistent preferences for cross-sex roles in make believe play or persistent fantasies of being the other sex.

- Intense desire to participate in the stereotypical games and pastimes of the other sex.

- Strong preference for playmates of the other sex.

B. Persistent discomfort with his or her sex or sense of inappropriateness in the gender role of that sex.

C. The disturbance is not **concurrent** with physical **intersex** condition.

D. The disturbance causes clinically significant distress or impairment in social, occupational, or other important areas of functioning.

Because one can experience confusion and questioning about gender identity at different stages of life, assessing whether someone has GID requires long-term monitoring during all developmental stages. It is a rare condition that occurs in only about one in every 54,000 people.

GID and Young Children

Boys and girls suspected with GID exhibit cross-gender identification symptoms in a similar manner. Both want to wear the clothing of the other gender. Boys will even improvise when female clothing is not available, using towels for skirts or to represent long hair, for example. Girls will often want their hair cut extremely short and only wear male or unisex clothing; when they do, they are often mistaken for boys. Both boys and girls may participate in activities traditionally expected of the other. For example, boys may enjoy playing house and will assume the role of mother. Girls who exhibit GID will play rough games and sports most often played by boys their age. Their favorite playmates are usually of the opposite sex. The heroes of boys with GID will likely be female, including Barbie® and other female characters; girls will most likely look toward male superheroes as their heroes.

As specified in the DSM-IV, children with GID also exhibit discomfort with their biological sex. Boys may insist on sitting down when urinating, and girls may attempt to stand to do so. It is not unusual for boys with GID to state that they hate their penis and testicles, and that they will eventually fall off or have them removed, to be replaced by a vagina. Girls may believe they will grow a penis when they get older and insist that they don't want to develop breasts or menstruate.

Remember, not all children who exhibit some of these characteristics can be diagnosed with GID. For some, the fascination with the opposite gender identity is a passing phase. For others, it can continue into adolescence and beyond.

Little boys and girls learn their gender roles at very young ages. Those with gender identity disorder will be uncomfortable with these stereotyped roles.

GID *and* Adolescents

When a child enters adolescence, establishing a diagnosis of GID can be even more difficult. The teenage years bring with them a new sense of independence. This newly found freedom can lead to experimentation in many facets of life. Teens often hold in their most guarded secrets, and these include any doubts they might have about their gender identity. Parents and teachers may sense that "something" is wrong, but not have any idea what is causing the teen distress. Only when the teen exhibits **overt** cross-dressing behaviors can a suspicion of GID be formed and a diagnosis made.

Adolescents and adults with GID sometimes tell their closest friends and relatives that they want to be the other sex. They often have the desire to live and be treated as the opposite sex, often passing as such. Convinced that they are physically the wrong sex, adolescents and adults with GID may become preoccupied with ridding themselves of their sexual characteristics. Males may ask for hormones to increase breast size. Girls may ask for testosterone and other male hormones to deepen their voices, build muscle, and grow body hair. Males may want surgery to remove a penis and testicles, or girls may ask for mastectomies.

Great care needs to be taken when considering a diagnosis of GID or other gender disorder not to confuse a dissatisfaction with a culture's definition of gender role with gender identity. Television shows from the 1950s and 1960s could give one the impression that women were only wives and mothers, teachers, and nurses. When a woman was shown participating in another career, she was often looked upon with suspicion. For many years, it was considered inappropriate for women to wear pants, and in some parts of society, it is still frowned on or even prohibited.

For the most part, cultural **stereotypes** about what is gender acceptable have fallen by the wayside. To make that happen, it was necessary for individuals to fight for change, bravely standing up to long-held beliefs and *archaic* practices. The fact that these individuals—male and female—did not follow cultural norms for their sex does not mean they had any form of gender identity issues. Their issues were with society and its restrictions.

Chapter 5
The Mother of All Bad Days

ye, Mom. I'll try and have dinner fixed when you get home."

"You don't have to cook tonight, you have your homework to do, and—"

"There's a new recipe for shrimp scampi I want to try," I interrupt. "And cooking will be a nice break."

"Okay then, honey, see you later."

A peck on the cheek, a wave, and Mom's on her way.

It's easier to say good-bye in the mornings now, two weeks after starting at Shore View. Ms. Torres got me out of gym class, so I can avoid the real chamber of horrors. I've managed to stay away from Cain Williams; I just give him wide berth. I've also found out about the red-haired surfer kid: his name's Dirk and he's a dropout. So again, I avoid him and things work out okay.

I still don't trust any of the students here. I'm not that stupid. But I make small talk with Vanna, Josh, Ashley, and Tanya between classes at my locker. It's like I've made a little picket fence in our relationships, where we can meet and chat but not cross over. Rather pleasant, really.

Ms. Torres suggested we talk regularly, and I've stopped in several more times. She appears genuinely interested in my musings and experiences, and I am more than grateful for an empathetic person.

So things are okay.

So far.

I walk to my locker and spin the dials; I hardly have to look to get that lock open now.

Funny, I don't see Vanna and her clique. Where could they be? This is odd.

Oh, well. Off to class. I make the way down the hall toward Earth Science. Hmm . . . the other kids seem to get strangely quiet as I walk past them. No one says 'hello,' no one looks me in the eye.

In fact, I swear that girl just turned her back on me.

Something strange is going on here.

Well, here's Mr. V's room: nothing to do but go in. I still have my own lab space, so I just do my thing and write down notes. No one talks to me, and I return the favor. An uneventful hour.

Second period: history of film class. I take my normal seat. Tanya nods. "Hey, Kevin."

"Hey, Tanya. What's our movie today?"

"*Psycho*—the original Hitchcock version."

Just what I needed—spooky movie for a really weird morning. It seems like I have a big spot on me or something, the way everyone's acting strange when I walk by. I want to ask, 'Hey Tanya, what's going on here?' But I don't know her well enough.

Third period: study hall. Megan Sommers, head of the cheerleading squad, sits on my side of the table. When the supervisor is looking the other way, she slides down toward me. "Kevin, is it true?"

"Is what true?"

"Well . . . maybe I should call you, *Kendra?*"

I just about fall off my chair. "Where'd you hear that?"

Megan slips a piece of paper into my hand. On the top is a Web address, and beneath that the words, *The Kyle Report: All the Dirt on Shore View High.* I've heard of Kyle Brown's blog; he's the geekiest kid at the school, but he exercises some sort of weird power by hosting this site that airs all the school gossip. I have a really bad feeling.

My hands are shaking, the room seems to be spinning. I close my eyes, pull air in, make my eyes focus. Then I force myself to read the printed article. The title screams at me: *Shore View Trannie.*

Strange but true, newly transferred Shore View senior Kevin Campbell is (or was) at his (her) old school known as KENDRA Campbell. So he's a she! Or is she a he? I know, I know—this is too bizarre to believe. Okay, here's the evidence. A star athlete at this school (name withheld) has a cousin at Pine Cove High, which is up the coast in Central CA. This cousin swears up and down that EVERYONE at Pine Cove knew Kevin—er, Kendra—and he/she made a big deal in his/her last semester there about really being a girl. You can talk to anyone at that school and they'll tell you—it's really true. So, we already have our share of fags and lesbos, but now we have our very own she-male right here in Surf City. Next time you see Kevin—er, Kendra—be sure and tell him—er, her—hello from the Kyle Report.

My heart feels like it's stopped.
I glance back at Megan. "Everyone knows?"
"*Everyone.*"

"The whole school?"

"Pretty much."

Still grasping the article, I jump up from my chair, steady myself for an instant to overcome dizziness, and run out of the room. I hear a chorus of laughter behind me.

I race down the empty halls to my locker. Gotta' get my stuff and get out of this school now. I round the corner, and—

There's a sign taped on my locker. Huge red letters on poster-board: *Kendra's Locker.*

I stagger toward the sign, rip it off. My head is swimming, the room spins. Then . . . nothing, only blackness. . . .

When I open my eyes, the first thing I notice is that my forehead hurts.

Where am I? White cabinets, medicine smell, a thin pillow under my head: I'm in the nurse's office.

"How's the head feel? You took a nasty fall."

I turn my gaze to the side, slowly. Ms. Torres is sitting next to me, concern on her face.

"The pain in my head isn't too bad. But that's not the worst of it," I tell her.

She nods. "I found this in the hallway, where you fell." She's holding the *Kyle Report.* "Do you know if many students have read this?"

"I'm afraid it's all over the school."

"I'm not surprised. Gossip travels at the speed of light." She pauses a moment, then changes the subject. "I've called your mom. We were pretty concerned when you passed out in the hall."

"I'm glad she's coming." And I mean it.

"Until she gets here, rest up," Ms. Torres tells me.

A few minutes later, Mom arrives. When Ms. Torres shows her the Internet article, I can tell Mom's heart is almost as broken as mine.

"Mom, Ms. Torres, I can't go to this school any longer."

The two women look at me.

"Are you sure?" Mom asks.

"Of course I'm sure. Are you kidding? I can't face the kids here. The whole school's against me."

"And what will happen at the next school?" Ms. Torres asks.

"I'll start over fresh."

"And the school after that?"

I bite my lip and scowl. "You're saying I can't run away from my problems, I have to work through them where I am. Right?"

They don't have to answer: I know.

"Let's try this," Ms. Torres suggests. "Try to stay two more weeks at Shore View. Whenever you feel really uncomfortable in class or anywhere on campus, you can cut-out and see me in my office. I'll give you all the help and support I can to help you cope with your peers. Who knows? You might receive more acceptance from other students than you expect. After two weeks, you evaluate the situation. If you want to leave for another school at that point, I'll give you my blessing." The counselor turns to my mom. "Mrs. Campbell, what do you think of that?"

"Sounds good to me, but it's not really my decision."

I suck in a deep breath. "I'll do it," I tell them both. "I'll give Shore View two more weeks."

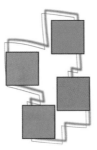

GID Treatment

When it comes to treatment, options center on behavior modification. According to psychologist Anne Vitale, treatment of GID requires a three-staged approach.

Stage I: Evaluation, Diagnosis, Individual/Group Psychotherapy, Education
   In this stage, the individual with suspected GID is thoroughly evaluated, both physically and

When a woman feels like a man or a man feels like a woman, there are a variety of treatment options that may be explored. Cross-dressing is one of the possibilities that may make an individual feel more at home in her/his body.

psychologically. The individual is also assessed for the potential of self-destructive behavior as well as whether he or she is self-medicating with hormones.

Psychotherapy is used to help the person find effective ways of living. It also provides the person with education on alternative ways to live, with realistic goals and means to alleviate stress. Some of the effective ways of living include cross-dressing in the underwear of the opposite sex or unisexually; removal of body hair; breast binding in the case of females; and participation in support groups.

Stage II: Hormone Replacement Therapy

Not everyone diagnosed with GID feels that it is necessary to undergo hormone therapy, but for those that do, the individual is referred to a doctor who can prescribe the hormones. Along with the hormone treatments, continuing visits with a psychotherapist are often recommended to help deal with the body's changes.

During Stage II, the decision to transition into the opposite sex is generally made. Not everyone will decide to do this; some will be content with the effects brought on by hormone replacement therapy. For those who decide to undergo sexual reassignment surgery, treatment includes support as the individual begins living full time in a new gender in preparation for surgery and in the necessary tasks of getting a new driver's license, changing status on Social

Security forms, and in educating the individual's friends and family about the change.

Stage III: Reassignment Surgery
While living as the opposite sex during the preoperative stage, some will find that the change is too difficult, and they will decide against having the surgery. Others, however, will choose to continue on to have the surgery. Letters from two mental-health professionals trained in the treatment of GID are necessary before surgery can proceed. After surgery,

The physical transformation into the opposite sex should be a gradual process, allowing the individual time to assess whether this is the right course of action.

A person at stage III in GID treatment may live for a time as a member of the opposite sex, wearing clothes, wigs, or makeup that will make others perceive this individual as the opposite sex. This in-between period before reassignment surgery helps the individual determine whether or not this transformation is too difficult to live out in daily life.

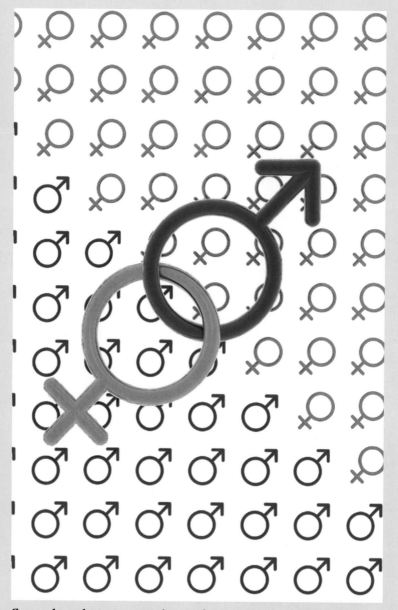

Sex and gender are topics that evoke strong emotions. North Americans are often offended by or at least uncomfortable with any blurring of the lines between male and female, feminine and masculine.

psychotherapy continues to provide support to the individual cope with a new life.

GID and Gender Confusion Treatment in Children and Adolescents

Children are generally brought into treatment because parents are alarmed at their child's behavior. They gave birth to a boy or girl, but this infant has grown into a child with little or no interest in what a boy (or girl) is traditionally interested in. Or, perhaps a parent or teacher is concerned because the child is the focus of constant teasing from peers. In either case, making a diagnosis of GID should be done cautiously. For the younger child, it must be kept in mind that such behaviors can be a phase, something the child will go through and then grow out of. For teens, adolescence is a time of experimentation, and that should be kept in mind as well.

Many children do not meet the official criteria for a diagnosis of GID, although they might exhibit some GID-type behaviors. As a result, medical and surgical treatments are generally ill advised in the case of children and adolescents. For most, behavior modification therapy is the treatment of choice. However, treatment of any sort is controversial; not everyone agrees it is necessary or even desirable.

There are many branches of behavior modification, but generally, they are based on the practice of using a system of rewards and punishments to promote good behaviors and eliminate less desirable ones.

What is considered gender-appropriate clothing and behaviors vary from culture to culture and era to era. For example, in most North American circles, if a man wears a skirt, he would be considered to be cross-dressing. But no one would consider the Scottish gentleman in this photo to be feminine! Today, the kilt has become more popular for formal male attire in a wider circle of Western culture.

In the case of gender identity, when a child exhibits what might be considered "gender-appropriate" behaviors, he would be rewarded. For example, if a male child who gender identifies as a female exhibits such behaviors as crossing his legs or talking about lipstick, pretty dresses, and dolls, his therapist would turn away and do something else, as though he had absolutely no interest in what the boy said. If, however, this same child talks about football, cars, or other traditionally masculine topics, the therapist would pay attention to him, engaging him in conversation. Outside of therapy sessions, the child's mother would be encouraged to give him some small reward for masculine behavior and dress.

Some studies have found that more than 50 percent of male children experiencing gender-identity confusion do not have a father or other male figure in the home. In these cases, participation in a program such as Big Brothers can provide the male child with a role model for masculine behavior.

Again, it is important to remember that the definition of gender-appropriate behaviors is not static; it changes with time and culture. For example, men were the first to be employed as knitters. When machinery was built that allowed for the mass production of knitted garments, women became the primary knitters. Though most knitters today are women, increasing numbers of men are learning to knit for pleasure. In the world of cooking, for many years it was believed that women, although they cooked for their families, were unsuited to be chefs. That myth has changed as well.

GID *and* Pharmacological Treatments

Although there are no drugs to treat GID, there are some medications that can be used to treat conditions that arise. Peer pressure, stress, and other conditions that are a normal part of life can be overwhelming to someone with gender identity issues. For children and adolescents, this can be especially traumatic. Individuals who are different—for whatever reason—are often the brunt of teasing and bullying. This can lead to depression, a serious and life-threatening condition. Besides counseling on how to deal with the behaviors of others, some individuals can benefit from antidepressants, such as selective serotonin reuptake inhibitors (SSRIs). SSRIs, such as Zoloft®, inhibit the reuptake of the **neurotransmitter** serotonin, making more of it available in the brain. Serotonin affects mood and sleep patterns among other things. Taking an SSRI or other antidepressant can greatly assist someone dealing with depression.

Depression is not the only psychiatric disorder that someone with GID may experience. Studies indicate that depression and anxiety are the most common, with 71 percent of patients in one study experiencing a mood disorder or an anxiety disorder, but 45 percent of all patients with GID in this study also had substance-related disorders, 42 percent had personality disorders, 6.5 percent had psychotic disorders, and 3.2 percent had eating disorders.

Support Groups

Support groups exist for almost every condition imaginable, and that includes individuals with gender-identity issues. Through meeting with others dealing with the same issues, individuals can gain insight into how to better their lives. Methods of coping with everyday situations can be shared. Support groups cannot help people realize they are not so alone after all, since others share their same issues and challenges.

If someone is not comfortable in face-to-face group situations or cannot make it to meetings, the Internet offers opportunities for them to participate in support groups as well. Here, under the cloak of anonymity, individuals may feel more comfortable sharing their feelings and personal stories. However, when chatting on the Internet, one should be very careful about how much personal information is given. Although most people do not present a danger, there are some who use the Internet for unsavory reasons. One should never give out a complete name or address to anyone whose identity is unknown. Should one decide to meet someone in person, exercise caution: meet as part of a group and in a public place. If you keep these cautions in mind, participation in an online chat room or e-mail discussion list can be very beneficial.

Chapter 6

Pull-Down, Smack-Down

Why did I ever agree to this? The past two days have been worse than I ever imagined. Even the worst times at Pine Cove—and those were *bad*—were nothing like this.

Students either shun me, or they mock me. They stare at me like I'm a freak show act. A couple of times, Ashley and her friends tried to approach me at the locker, but I avoided them. Fact is, I kinda' like them—except for Josh—and I'm too afraid of facing their rejection along with the others'. That would be the final straw.

So it's me against Shore View High: not a very even match.

And old demons have returned to haunt me. When I'm alone at home, I'm tempted to start cutting again. I asked

Mom to hide all the razors and all the knives in the house, for fear of what I might do to myself. That presents a new problem: hair appears on my chin, and stubble protrudes under my armpits and on my legs. I hate hair on my body—but it's that or risk self-mutilation. How long can I keep the old temptations away?

It's lunchtime now, at school. I order my food from the fast-food vendor in the school cafeteria, and then I take my tray with burger and fries out the back door of the main building. There's an alcove back here, with a bench seat surrounded by leafy bird-of-paradise plants. I sit on the bench and eat alone there, with the sunshine streaming down and little birds that chirp in the fronds. A sparrow hops around my feet, hoping for crumbs. I throw her little bits of my fries. I feel like that bird is my only friend.

"Who-oa, it's the Shore View she-male!"

That voice freezes the blood in my veins. Cain.

I turn around, slowly, lest I reveal the extent of my terrible fear.

Cain and two of his buddies circle the bench, like a pack of wild animals preparing for a kill.

Cain stands in front of me, hands on hips. "So, Kevin …oh, I mean, Kendra—I don't get it. I mean, are you a boy or a girl? Really?"

I shut my eyes, try to focus my mind elsewhere. *Ignore them, they'll go away,* they told me when I was little.

It's not true.

"Guess we'll have to take a little look and figure this out for ourselves," Cain said with a nasty chuckle.

His two henchmen grab my arms from behind, yanking me up from the bench. Cain grabs my pants by the belt loops and yanks. I wince as the tight jeans scrape down my hips and fall at my feet.

There's nothing I can do, nothing at all. I'm completely helpless, vulnerable. I shut my eyes tight, trying to close out reality.

Then . . . *whomp.*

I open my eyes. Cain is holding the side of his face, a surprised and pained look on his face.

His companions let go of my arms. I quickly pull my pants back up. And then I see Josh.

He circles behind Cain, rubbing the back of his right fist with his left hand. Apparently, he just popped the bully on his jaw.

Cain sneers. "Boy Wonder, you just made a big mistake." The three move slowly toward him. "Let's get him, guys," Cain commands.

They start to throw punches. Josh blocks and swings back, but it's three against one.

I want to run away, but my legs are shaking too much. And I can't let this guy get pummeled after he tried to help me.

I reach into my back pocket . . . it's still there. Safety pins are a girl's best friend, they say. I straighten out the needle and run up behind Cain, bring down the needle in my fist. Right into his back.

The bully screams. Turns. Slaps me so hard I'm thrown to the ground, landing on my elbow.

He turns to his companions. "You guys take Josh. I'm gonna teach this trannie a lesson it'll never forget." He lunges toward me. . .

Thunk!

A shiny blue, knee-length boot with stiletto heel flies from behind me and nails Cain in the face. "Take that!" Vanna exclaims.

Cain moans and slumps on the pavement. His buddies turn their heads to see what's happening, giving Josh a moment to kick. One of Cain's thugs bends over, whimpering.

A whistle shrieks, making us all turn our heads. Mrs. Pao, campus security guard, comes running. She's shouting into her portable radio. Moments later, more staff arrive.

I'm safe.

I look at Josh and Vanna. She's panting, but she flashes me a triumphant smile. Josh has a nasty bruise swelling one eye, and an embarrassed look on his face. "I hate to be violent," he says. "I wish I'd thought of another solution."

"I'm just thankful for the one you came up with," I tell him. And then I sit back down on the bench and start to cry. Tears flow down my face; I don't know when I've cried so hard.

Vanna sits beside me, puts her arm over my shoulder. "Hey, it's okay. You're safe now. It's all over."

"Oh, Vanna, you don't understand," I tell her. "These are tears of happiness. You two—you both took a risk to rescue me. I just realized: I have real friends at this school!"

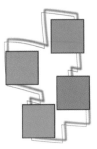

Real-Life Tragedy: Teena/Brandon

In 1999, actress Hilary Swank won an Academy Award® for her portrayal of Teena Brandon and Brandon Teena in a story that showed how cruel individuals can be.

Teena Brandon was born in Lincoln, Nebraska, in 1972. Although born female, Teena considered herself to be male for much of her life. When she was in high school, Teena would stuff rolled socks in the front of her pants, bind her breasts, call herself Billy, and date girls from other schools. She even got engaged to two girls. Teena didn't keep her masquerade a secret from everyone. Her mother knew that Teena believed she was a male, and Teena told some of her friends. But the more people she told, the more difficult things got for her.

Teena was not a model of good behavior. She became **adept** at lying, she stole, and she forged checks. Her criminal behavior made a bad situation worse, and in 1993, she decided to start a new life in a new town with a new identity—Brandon Teena.

Life for Brandon in the small Nebraska town of Humboldt seemed to be going well. People accepted Brandon, and he made many friends, male and female. He even fell in love. But though Brandon changed his location and his identity, he fell into Teena's old habits when he ran out of money. His forgery landed him in jail in December 1993, and his sex put him in the female section of the jail.

Brandon's stint in the Humboldt jail blew his cover as a male, especially when he was listed as being

For a person like Teena Brandon, filling out a simple form like this one presents a major identity challenge.

In order for a woman to be taken seriously in the business world, she must wear certain attire that is very similar to a man's. Imagine, however, if a businessman tried to earn respect by dressing like a woman! What does this tell you about North American culture and gender roles?

female in the town newspaper's story about his arrest. His girlfriend, Lana, confronted him, and Brandon told her that he was saving money to undergo sex reassignment surgery.

On Christmas Eve, Brandon and Lana attended a party with friends, including Tom Nissen and John Lotter. Nissen and Lotter decided to prove to Lana that Brandon was female, and prove to Brandon that "his kind" shouldn't be involved with Lana. After Lana left the party, Nissen beat and kicked Brandon. Afterward, Nissen and Lotter drove Brandon to a secluded area, where each raped him and then left him, coatless in the cold.

Although Nissen and Lotter had warned Brandon not to tell anyone of the attack, Lana convinced him to go to the hospital and call the sheriff. Sheriff Charles Laux took Brandon's statement, but his questions were directed more toward Brandon's lifestyle than the rape and assault. Reports indicate that the sheriff even referred to Brandon as "it." He questioned Brandon about his sexual experiences—including whether or not he was a virgin. Clearly, Sheriff Laux did not take Brandon's claims seriously.

A few days after Brandon signed a complaint against Nissen and Lotter, deputy sheriffs questioned the suspects and prepared to arrest them. However, Sheriff Laux would not authorize the arrest to take place, so they remained free.

Their freedom cost Brandon Teena his life. On December 30, Nissen and Lotter found Brandon at the home of Lisa Lambert. The pair murdered Teena, along with Lambert and a friend of Lambert's.

Lambert's baby son was left alone in the house with the bodies.

Nissen and Lotter were immediate suspects, and they were arrested the following afternoon. Both were convicted of the murders.

Sheriff Laux's lack of action in Brandon's rape and assault was met with disgust by many, including Brandon's mother, JoAnn Brandon. She filed a wrongful death suit against the sheriff, claiming that his mishandling of the rape and assault charges led to Brandon's death. Laux claimed he was trying to avoid a rush to judgment that might compromise any upcoming case. Although a lower Nebraska court

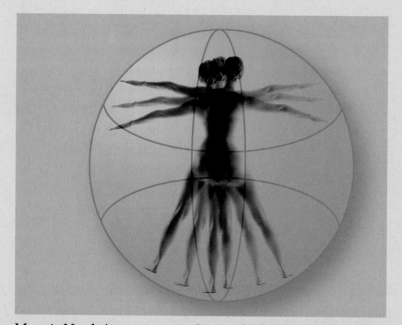

Many in North America are intolerant of individuals with gender issues. Prejudice and hatred make it even more difficult for these individuals to achieve a healthy sense of their own identities.

dismissed the suit, the Nebraska Supreme Court reinstated it, because the sheriff had told Nissen and Lotter about the complaint but had not offered Brandon protection. The lower court found in favor of Brandon's mother and awarded her approximately $17,000. Again, the Nebraska Supreme Court stepped in, ruling that the amount was too little and ordered that it be increased.

Gender-Identity Issues and the School

For many children and adolescents, being teased or bullied makes up a large part of the day. Some students either **feign** illness or actually become sick to avoid their tormentors at school. Children and adolescents with gender-identity issues are frequent targets of violence and taunts at school.

Difficulties faced by students with gender-identity issues have not gone unnoticed by many schools and professional organizations, including the American School Counselor Association (ASCA). In 1995, the group issued its first position statement on dealing with gay, lesbian, bisexual, transgendered, and questioning (GLBTQ) youth; the statement was revised in 2000 and 2005. As stated on their Web site http://www.schoolcounselor.org/content.asp?contentid=217, the role of professional school counselors is to promote equal opportunity and respect for all individuals regardless of sexual orientation or gender identity. Professional school counselors work to eliminate barriers that impede student development and achievement and are committed to academic, personal/social, and career development of all students.

Professional school counselors realize these issues [bullying, harassment] may infringe upon healthy student development and limit their opportunities in school and the community.

The official ASCA position calls on school counselors to:

- assist students as they clarify feelings about their own sexual orientation/gender identity and the identity of others in a nonjudgmental manner.

Gender identity is particularly important to adolescents who are working to find their own sense of who they are. Teenagers may want to experiment with various possibilities—but at the same time, not conforming to the norm can lead to discrimination and harassment.

- advocate for **equitable** educational opportunities for all students.

- address inappropriate language from students and adults.

- promote sensitivity and acceptance of diversity among all students and staff.

- provide GLBTQ-inclusive and age-appropriate information on issues such as diverse family structures, dating and relationships, and sexually transmitted diseases.

- model language that is inclusive of sexual orientation/gender identity.

- encourage policies that address discrimination against any student.

- promote violence-prevention activities to create a safe school environment that is free of fear, bullying, and hostility.

The ASCA also asks school counselors to help GLBTQ students gain self-acceptance, deal with social acceptance, understand everything involved in "coming out," and identify resources in the community that might be of benefit to them.

Chapter 7

Happy Ending—
At Least for Now

t's a full-moon night, creating the perfect combination of tide and wave-motion for nocturnal surfing. There've been some changes in my life since that day two months ago when Josh and Vanna came to my rescue. The silvery moonlight reflects off my hair, longer now than it used to be, and off the shiny pink hibiscus pattern on my favorite surfboard, and the glassy surface of the ocean around me.

I hear a rushing sound from seaward, a big wave, taller than I've seen in a while, a perfectly shaped wall of water cutting from west to east across the horizon. I paddle like mad, hop up, and absorb the initial shock of energy from the wave. Then I'm on the lip, cutting down into the tube.

A vortex of water and spray whirls around me for a few exhilarating moments before I shoot out of the curl and bounce on the board, creating buoyancy to bring me all the way into the shore.

There's a blazing bonfire ahead of me on the beach where my friends are. I ride to where the ocean laps at the sand, take my board under my arm, and walk into the warmth and light surrounding the blaze.

Josh and Ashley are reclining on one blanket, sipping sodas and smiling at each other. Vanna's in a fold-out chair, carefully brushing off any sand that blows on her. She won't go in the water—"Too messy," she says—but she likes to hang out with the others on the beach. Tanya is on another blanket, playing cards with Nura, an Afghani girl that Tanya met at the library where she volunteers as a tutor. She's teaching Nura how to play spit.

Three other students swap jokes on the other side of the fire. There's Jada, whom I'm happy to say has broken free of her relationship with Cain Williams. Cain is now in juvenile hall, waiting to be sentenced for an attempted assault. Sitting near Jada is the red-haired terror of the beach, Dirk, whom I hear is trying to reform his life. (Jury's still out on that endeavor.) He's laughing with Keisha Arellano, the teen girls surfboard champion, a new friend of his.

I amble over and set my board down on the sand, between Josh and Vanna. "Hey, where's Jason?" I ask the Asian princess, referring to her new flame, a punk rocker of local fame.

"He has a gig tonight down in Anaheim. He's gonna' pick up Ethan and Bob, and join us later."

I sit on the board and stare into the fire. My heart feels as warm as the leaping flames; I've never had so many people my own age that I could relax and enjoy hanging out with.

Josh looks my way. "You know, Kev—I mean, Kendra— sorry, takes a little getting used to the new name."

"That's okay, Josh. I'm still getting used to it myself."

He smiles. "I was gonna say, Kendra, that's a pretty hip board you've got there."

"C'mon, Josh, macho guy like you. You don't have to say that."

"No, for real. Roxy makes good sticks. Clean, classic lines, and that Hawaiian flower pattern on the top looks real vintage, too. If I was a chick, I'd run downtown and buy one of those boards for myself."

"Well, Josh," I grin, "you could get in touch with your feminine side and buy one anyway. Give the locals something to talk about."

"Uh . . . no."

Laughs around the fire.

"Hard to believe, but we're gonna graduate before you know it," Vanna says.

"Where'd that come from?" I ask.

"Just staring at the fire, thinking about life."

"I don't want to think too much about that," I tell her. "I'm happy with life now."

"Oh, come on," she retorts. "You have to be thinking some about life after graduation. I'll miss Shore View, but we'll all keep in touch, even if we go separate ways. Life will keep on getting better and better." That's Vanna, always looking on the rosy side.

"So, Kendra, what are your plans for the future?" Ashley asks, leaning over Josh's torso.

"Well ... I'm not so focused on schools like most of you are. There are some other things I want to work on before I set my academic goals."

"Things like ... ?" Vanna asks.

"Really basic stuff, like my identity. I've never been in touch with myself, because I was too scared trying to survive the peer pressure. But you've all given me something I never had—your friendship allows me to like myself. Maybe now I can safely explore who I am."

"Deep," Josh intones, and everyone laughs.

"Traditionally, my people would refer to you as a *nadleeh*, Kendra," Tanya pipes up.

"What does 'nadleeh' mean?"

"It means 'one who walks two paths'—the male and female paths—through life," the Navajo girl replied. "There's a long tradition of this in my culture, going back for hundreds of years."

"So Native Americans understood there would be people like me?" I find that thought really interesting, and reassuring somehow.

"Yes, at least the Diné did. I'm not sure about other tribes."

Vanna leans forward to look into my face. "Are you planning to have a sex change operation?"

"That's a possibility," I tell her. "Once I'm an adult, I'll have the freedom to change my body to conform to my mind—if that's what I want. But I'm not sure. It's a huge decision, bigger than choices most people ever make. I could do that, or go with hormone therapy, or maybe just be happy the way I am." I pause for a moment, and then I add, "Who knows? Maybe someday I'll want to be Kevin again. It's confusing."

"Well, whatever you do, whoever you are, you'll still be my friend," Vanna says. Heads nod around the bonfire.

I smile and stare at the flames, watching them turn blue at the tips and send sparks swirling toward the stars. My future won't be simple, I know that. I was made more complex than most people are, so I'll probably continue to be an enigma, even to myself.

But as long as I have friends, the future seems as bright as the full moon over the ocean.

Being "macho" is one way young men conform to their socially accepted gender role.

GID Controversy

Not everyone agrees that GID is actually a disorder. Although GID is listed as one in DSM-IV-TR, there are those who argue against its inclusion. Some opponents of the concept of GID as a disorder claim that GID is a pre-homosexual condition, and since homosexuality is no longer listed as a psychiatric disorder (it was removed from the DSM in 1973), then its **precursor**, child and adolescent GID, should not be considered one either. Some opponents of its inclusion as a disorder believe that labeling it as one gives the **connotation** that something about the

If a little boy enjoys playing house, should he be considered "abnormal"? In today's world, where gender roles are changing, such a categorization would be particularly inappropriate. Many experts, however, say that GID should never be considered a disorder but merely an alternative way of living in the world.

individual is wrong, that it is broken and must be fixed. For them, GID is another way of living or a biological condition.

But what about GID and homosexuality? Without a doubt, some people with GID are homosexual—just as a certain percentage of the population without GID is homosexual. Having a diagnosis of GID or other gender-identity issues does not mean that someone is a homosexual.

But what about a woman with GID who has a sexual relationship with another woman, or a man with another man, doesn't that make them homosexual? No. Remember the definition of gender identity: gender is determined by the individual. To someone born as a female but whose gender identity is male, having a relationship with a woman would not be considered a same-sex relationship.

Living as Someone with GID

As one's body takes on defining male or female characteristics, it may no longer conform to how the individual had identified herself. This *incongruity* can manifest in transsexual or transgender behaviors. Although they share some common characteristics, they are not the same things.

Transsexual

Individuals who identify themselves as being transsexuals have the desire to live as the opposite sex in every way. After a period of living as the other gender and undergoing hormone therapy, most go on to have sex reassignment surgery, thereby permanently

GID is not the same as homosexuality. A gay male may be quite comfortable being masculine, just as a lesbian female may enjoy her femininity.

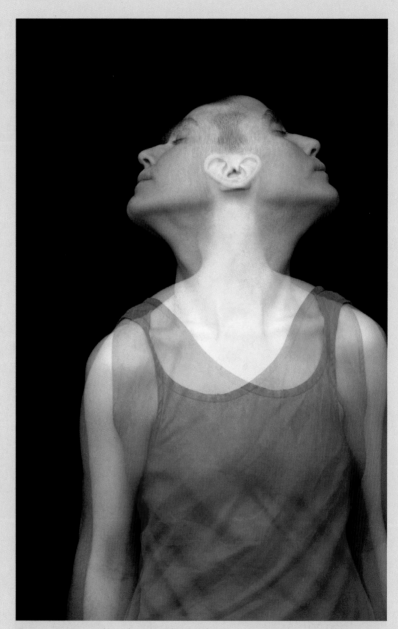

Some transgendered individuals choose not to identify themselves as either male or female. In effect, they look in both directions, incorporating masculine and feminine by adopting an appearance that is gender neutral.

changing their sex. Sexual reassignment to female from male is more common than the reverse.

Transgender

Someone who identifies himself as transgendered assumes the role of the opposite sex, but seldom undergoes sex reassignment surgery. Some do choose to take hormones to make their appearance more like that of the other sex. This is also called dual-role transvestism.

Included in the transgender category are individuals who like to crossdress. Crossdressers (formerly called transvestites) do not desire to live as the opposite sex, take hormones, or undergo sex reassignment surgery. They simply enjoy dressing up in clothing—and in the case of men crossdressing as women, using the makeup—of the opposite sex. Contrary to what appears in film and television, crossdressers seldom leave home dressed in full regalia. Theirs is a hidden life, away from friends and family. Crossdressing is not uncommon in children, and if caught and teased, they can bury their desires for many years. These activities often resurface during adulthood.

Others choose not to identify with either sex; they choose to live an **androgynous** lifestyle as much as possible. They may wear unisex clothing and adopt unisex hairstyles. This is the choice of some young adults, and at least one college—Oberlin in Ohio—provides facilities, including "gender-neutral" restrooms, to encourage their acceptance. Most young people who live an androgynous lifestyle will eventually adopt either a male or female identity.

Glossary

adept: Highly skillful.

amygdala: The part of the brain associated with feelings of fear and aggression.

androgynous: Neither male nor female in appearance.

archaic: No longer in general use.

cerebellum: The part of the brain that controls and coordinates muscular activity and maintains balance.

circumcised: Removed all or part of the foreskin from the penis.

concurrent: Occurring at the same time.

connotation: The implying or suggesting of an additional meaning for a word or phrase.

corpus callosum: The band of nerve fibers that connects the two hemispheres of the brain.

correlation: A relationship in which two or more things are mutual or in which one is caused by the other.

Diagnostic and Statistical Manual of Mental Disorders: A manual published by the American Psychiatric Association that covers all mental health disorders, the known causes of these disorders, statistics in terms of gender, age at onset, and prognosis, and optimal treatment approaches.

120

equitable: Fair.

feign: To make up something.

hermaphroditism: To have the condition in which an organism has the characteristics of both sexes.

hypothalamus: The part of the brain that controls involuntary functions, including the release of hormones.

hypothyroidism: A condition in which thyroid hormones are deficient, leading to a slowing of the metabolic rate.

incongruity: Something that doesn't seem to fit in with its context.

intersex: An organism with characteristics of both sexes.

neurotransmitter: Any one of a number of chemicals that are used to transmit nerve signals across a synapse.

overt: Out in the open; obvious.

phalloplasty: Reconstruction of the penis.

precursor: Something that came before and led to the development of another thing.

puberty: The developmental stage when an organism becomes capable of sexual reproduction.

sonograms: Graphical representation of sound.

stereotypes: Oversimplified ideas held by one person or group about another person or group.

testosterone: A male hormone produced in the testicles and responsible for the development of secondary sex characteristics.

Further Reading

Abrahams, George, and Sheila Ahlbrand. *Boy v. Girl: How Gender Shapes Who We Are, What We Want, and How We Get Along.* Minneapolis, Minn.: Free Spirit, 2002.

Colapinto, John. *As Nature Made Him: The Boy Who Was Raised as a Girl.* New York: Harper, 2001.

Huegel, Kelly. *GLBTQ: The Survival Guide for Queer and Questioning Teens.* Minneapolis, Minn.: Free Spirit, 2003.

Ojeda, Auriana. *Opposing Viewpoints: Male/Female Roles.* Farmington Hills, Mich.: Greenhaven, 2004.

Rich, Jason. *Growing Up Gay in America.* Madison, Wis.: Franklin Street Books, 2002.

Winfield, Cynthia L. *Gender Identity: The Ultimate Teen Guide.* Lanham, Md.: Scarecrow Press, 2006.

For More Information

Gender Identity Disorder
www.drkoop/ency/93/001527.html

Gender Public Advocacy Coalition
www.gpac.org

Mermaids: Family Support Group for Children and
Teenagers with Gender Identity Issues
www.mermaids.freeuk.com

Planned Parenthood Guide for Teens & Families
www.plannedparenthood.org/sexual-health/teenshealth/
guide-for-teens-and-families.htm.

Sex, etc.
www.sexetc.org

Sexual and Gender Orientation
www.sexualityandu.ca/teens/orientation.aspx

What Is Gender?
www.ppnyc.org/new/img/what_is_gender.pdf

Youth Resource
www.youthresource.com

Publisher's note:
The Web sites listed on this page were active at the time of publication. The publisher
is not responsible for Web sites that have changed their addresses or discontinued
operation since the date of publication. The publisher will review and update the
Web-site list upon each reprint.

Bibliography

Advocates for Youth. "Tips and Strategies for Taking Steps to Cultural Fairness." http://www.advocatesforyouth.org/publications/frtp/culturalfairness.htm.

American School Counselor Association. "Position Statement: Gay, Lesbian, Bisexual, Transgendered and Questioning Youth." http://www.schoolcounselor.org/content.asp?contentid=217.

Bauchner, Elizabeth. "The Pink Aisle: Toying with Stereotypes." http://www.tolerance.org/news/article_tol.jus?id=906.

"Gay, Lesbian, & Bisexual Issues." http://www.health24.com/sex/Gay_lesbian_bisexual_issues/1253-2462,32564.asp.

National Institute on Media and the Family. "Media's Effect on Girls: Body Image and Gender Identity." http://www.mediafamily.org/facts/facts_mediaeffect.shtml.

Ponton, Lynn. "From Laramie to California." http://dir.salon.com/story/mwt/col/pont/2002/11/11/pontonmon/index.html.

"Psychology of Gender Identity & Transgenderism." http://www.genderpsychology.org.

Ramsland, Katherine. "A Grisly Find." *Crime Library*. http://www.crimelibrary.com/classics4/brandon.

Rekers, George. "Gender Identity Disorder." http://www.leaderu.com/jhs/rekers.html.

Viatle, Anne. "Notes on Gender Role Transition." http://www.avitale.com.

Williams, Dana. "Caroline Is a Boy." http://www.tolerance.org/teach/magazine/features.jsp?&is=36&ar=564.

Williams, Dana. "What Transgender Means." http://www.tolerance.org/parents/kidsarticle.jsp?&=29.

Index

Picture Credits

iStockphoto: pp. 20, 54, 57, 88, 102, 117, 118
      Ahvo, Janne: p. 36
      Bayley, Don: p. 115
      Bendjy, Daniel: p. 69
      Bro, Helle: p. 21
      Dala, Anna Liza: p. 17
      Habur, Izabela: p. 70
      Kaulitzki, Sebastian: p. 58
      Large, Timothy: p. 68
      Lugaresi, Michele: p. 19
      Mullins, Meredith: p. 39
      Novakovic, Darko: p. 40
      Rich, Andrew: p. 73
      Schade, Michael: p. 114
      Struthers, Karen: p. 87
      Tchernov, Andrei: p. 101
      Volodin, Andrey: p. 35
Jupiter Images: pp. 84, 86, 104, 106

Authors

Kenneth McIntosh is a freelance writer living in northern Arizona with his family. He has written two dozen educational books, and taught at junior high, high school, and community college levels.

Ida Walker is a graduate of the University of Northern Iowa in Cedar Falls. She attended graduate school at Syracuse University in Syracuse, New York. She lives and works in Upstate New York.

Series Consultants

Andrew M. Kleiman, M.D., received a Bachelor of Arts degree in philosophy from the University of Michigan, and earned his medical degree from Tulane University School of Medicine. Dr. Kleiman completed his internship, residency in psychiatry, and a fellowship in forensic psychiatry at New York University and Bellevue Hospital. He is currently in private practice in Manhattan, specializing in psychopharmacology, psychotherapy, and forensic psychiatry. He also serves as an instructor of clinical psychiatry at the New York University School of Medicine.

Cindy Croft, M.A.Ed., is the Director of the Center for Inclusive Child Care (CICC) at Concordia University, St. Paul, MN. The CICC is a comprehensive resource network for promoting and supporting inclusive early childhood and school-age programs and providers with Project EXCEPTIONAL training and consultation, and other resources at www.inclusivechildcare. org. In addition to working with the CICC, Ms. Croft is on the faculty at Concordia University and Minneapolis Community and Technical College.